D0712923

Strange ... But True?

BIGFOOT

ELIZABETH NOLL

BLACK
RABBIT
BOOKS

Bolt is published by Black Rabbit Books
P.O. Box 3263, Mankato, Minnesota, 56002.
www.blackrabbitbooks.com
Copyright © 2017 Black Rabbit Books

Design and Production by Brad Norr and
Michael Sellner
Photo Research by Rhonda Milbrett

Library of Congress Control Number: 2015954920

HC ISBN: 978-1-68072-020-4   PB ISBN: 978-1-68072-290-1

Printed in the United States at CG Book Printers,
North Mankato, Minnesota, 56003. PO #1795 4/16

Contents

CHAPTER 1

Something's in the Woods

The setting sun glowed behind the trees. Rosie stood on the porch. As it got dark, she tried to turn on the light. The bulb was burned out.

Then Rosie saw a strange creature. It was 8 feet (2.4 meters) tall. "It turned and looked at me while it was walking," Rosie said.

She ran inside and called her dad. "I think I saw a Bigfoot!"

BIGFOOT SIGHTINGS IN THE UNITED STATES
(as of August 2015)

Washington
California
Florida
Illinois

606   428   306   270

Mysterious Animal

Thousands of people say they have seen a Bigfoot. They describe the beasts as giant, **furry** animals that walk on two legs.

But many other people say Bigfoot is just a story.

Another name for a Bigfoot is "Sasquatch."

Ohio	Oregon	Texas	Michigan	Georgia	Colorado
257	242	205	201	126	121

620
520
420
320
220
120

A GLOBE OF GIANTS

People around the world tell stories of ape-like creatures.

BIGFOOT (UNITED STATES)

MARICOXI (BRAZIL)

KALA BANDAR
(INDIA)

YETI
(HIMALAYAS)

YEREN
(CHINA)

ORANG PENDEK
(INDONESIA)

YOWIE
(AUSTRALIA)

CHAPTER 2

All about Bigfoot

In 1958, a **logger** in California found strange footprints. They were 16 inches (41 centimeters) long. Word of the footprints spread. One reporter called the footprints' owner "Bigfoot."

In the 1960s and 1970s, more people found giant footprints. And more people said they saw the creatures. People began to search for Bigfoot.

Describing Bigfoot

Researchers say a Bigfoot is 6 to 12 feet (2 to 4 m) tall. It weighs up to 1,000 pounds (454 kilograms). Witnesses say it is covered in fur and is very smelly.

People say Bigfoot creatures sometimes throw rocks. They might scream or **howl**. But they are also **shy**. They run away from people.

How much does a Bigfoot eat?

A small Bigfoot would need about 7,200 calories a day. That would be about 24 slices of pizza.

HOW BIG IS BIGFOOT?

GIRAFFE
17 FEET (5.2 M)

BIGFOOT
12 FEET (3.7 M)

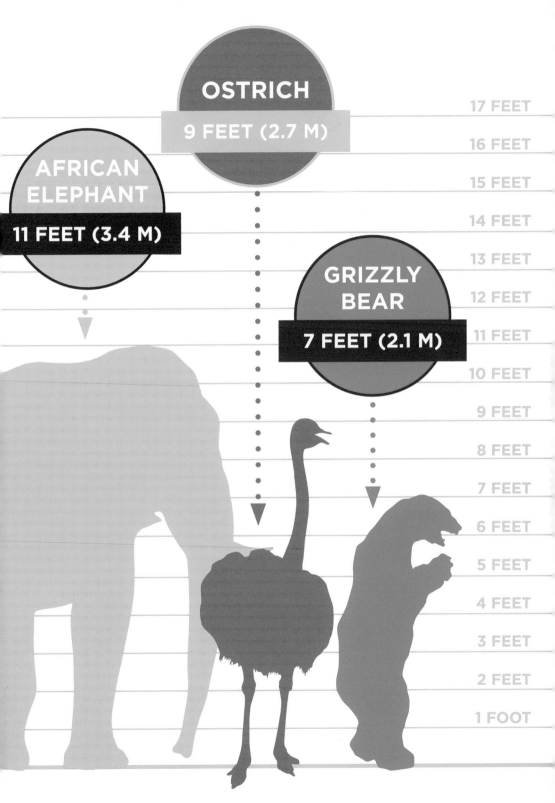

OSTRICH
9 FEET (2.7 M)

AFRICAN ELEPHANT
11 FEET (3.4 M)

GRIZZLY BEAR
7 FEET (2.1 M)

17 FEET
16 FEET
15 FEET
14 FEET
13 FEET
12 FEET
11 FEET
10 FEET
9 FEET
8 FEET
7 FEET
6 FEET
5 FEET
4 FEET
3 FEET
2 FEET
1 FOOT

CHAPTER 3

Bigfoot Sightings

Researchers know of about 3,500 Bigfoot **sightings** in North America. A sighting means somebody saw or heard a Bigfoot. It could also mean they found extra-large footprints.

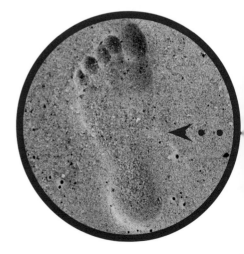

Bigfoot's Feet Would Be BIG

16 INCHES (41 CM)
BIGFOOT

11 INCHES (28 CM)
GRIZZLY BEAR

9.5 INCHES (24 CM)
AVERAGE 10-YEAR-OLD CHILD

BIGFOOT FEATURES

BAD TEMPER

LONG ARMS

FLATTENED FACE

DIRTY FUR

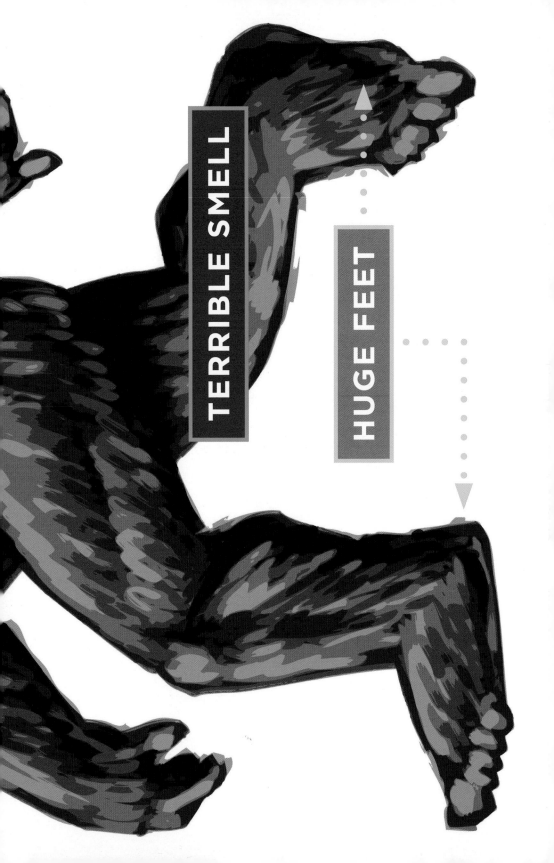

Was It a Bigfoot?

A man named Paul lived in the woods. One day, he saw huge **tracks** in the snow. The footprints led deep into the woods.

Paul's sister said she saw a hairy creature in the same place. The creature walked on two feet. They believe a Bigfoot lives in their woods.

Roger Patterson and Bob Gimlin claimed they filmed a Bigfoot in 1967. Later, a man investigated the movie. People told him the Bigfoot was a man in a fur suit. The truth is still a mystery.

Believing in Bigfoot

People all over the world tell tales about ape-men. Believers say these tales are so common they must be true.

Believers also look at photos, videos, and footprints. They say these items prove Bigfoot creatures are real.

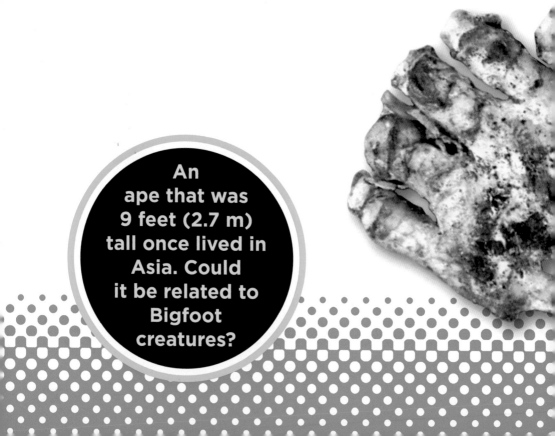

An ape that was 9 feet (2.7 m) tall once lived in Asia. Could it be related to Bigfoot creatures?

In 2012,
scientists tested fur believed
to be from Bigfoot creatures. All the fur
was from common animals, such as
cows, horses, and bears.

CHAPTER 4

Bigfoot Fakes

Other people disagree with believers. They say it's easy to make fake tracks and photos. The footprints that started the Bigfoot stories were fake. The logger used homemade wooden feet to make those tracks.

What Do You Think?

Some people say Bigfoot proof is weak. They ask why all the photos of them are **blurry**. They ask why the creatures only come out at night.

But those who believe think the photos are proof. They believe **witnesses'** stories.

Will the questions ever be answered?

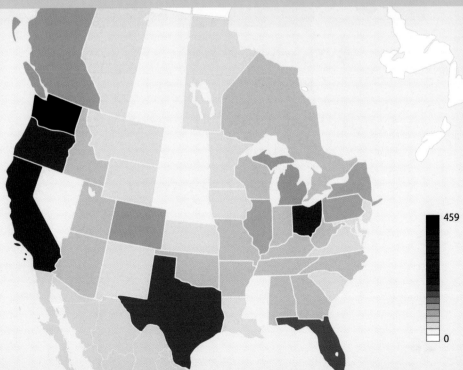

BEARFOOT?

Look at where American black bears live (top). Compare it to where Bigfoot sightings have been reported (bottom). Could the creatures be bears?

459

0

QUIZ

Believe It or Not?

Answer the questions below. Then add up your points to see if you believe.

1 **You see a big footprint in the mud. What do you think?**

A. That's not from any animal I know! (3 points)

B. That's odd. It's pretty big. (2 points)

C. I'm sure that's from a big boot. (1 point)

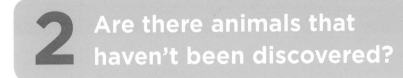

2 **Are there animals that haven't been discovered?**

A. Definitely! (3 points)

B. Maybe. (2 points)

C. There aren't monsters in the woods. (1 point)

3 **Look at the pictures in this book again. What do you think?**

A. I totally see a Bigfoot! (3 points)

B. What is that? (2 points)

C. That's totally fake! (1 point)

- - - - - - - - - - - -

3 points:
There's no way the creatures are real.

4–8 points:
Maybe they're real. But then again, maybe they're not.

9 points:
You're a total believer!

blurry (BLUR-ee)—not clear

film (FILM)—to make a movie

furry (FUR-ee)—covered in fur

howl (HOWL)—to make a long, loud cry that sounds sad

logger (LAH-gur)—someone who cuts down trees for wood

researcher (RE-surch-uhr)—someone who carefully studies something

shy (SHI)—feeling nervous about meeting new people

sighting (SIHT-ing)—spotting something

track (TRAK)—a mark left on the ground by an animal, person, or vehicle

witness (WIT-nes)—someone who sees something happen

BOOKS

Brockenbrough, Martha. *Finding Bigfoot: Everything You Need to Know.* New York: Feiwel and Friends, 2013.

Karst, Ken. *Bigfoot.* Enduring Mysteries. Mankato, MN: Creative Education, 2015.

Perish, Patrick. *Is Bigfoot Real?* Unexplained: What's the Evidence? Mankato, MN: Amicus, 2014.

Rivkin, Jennifer. *Searching for Bigfoot.* Mysterious Monsters. New York: PowerKids Press, 2015.

WEBSITES

The Bigfoot Field Researchers Organization
bfro.net

Finding Bigfoot: The Game
discoverykids.com/games/finding-bigfoot/

North America Bigfoot Search
nabigfootsearch.com/bigfootdescription.html

INDEX